Colors

Violet

Nancy Harris

Heinemann Library
Chicago, Illinois

HEINEMANN-RAINTREE

TO ORDER:
☎ Call Customer Service (Toll-Free) **1-888-454-2279**
💻 Visit **heinemannraintree.com** to browse our catalog and order online.

©2008 Heinemann-Raintree
a division of Pearson Education Limited
Chicago, Illinois

Editorial: Rebecca Rissman
Design: Kimberly R. Miracle and Joanna Hinton-Malivoire
Photo Research: Tracy Cummins and Tracey Engel
Production: Duncan Gilbert

Originated by Dot
Printed and bound by South China Printing Company
The paper used to print this book comes from sustainable resources.

ISBN-13: 978-1-4329-1592-6 (hc)
ISBN-10: 1-4329-1592-4 (hc)
ISBN-13: 978-1-4329-1602-2 (pb)
ISBN-10: 1-4329-1602-5 (pb)

12 11 10 09 08
10 9 8 7 6 5 4 3 2 1

**Library of Congress
Cataloging-in-Publication Data**

Harris, Nancy, 1956-
  Violet / Nancy Harris.
    p. cm. -- (Colors)
  Includes bibliographical references and index.
    ISBN 978-1-4329-1592-6 (hc) -- ISBN 978-1-4329-1602-2 (pb) 1.
Violet (Color)--Juvenile literature. 2. Color--Juvenile literature. I. Title.
QC495.5.H377 2008
535.6--dc22

                        2008005610

Acknowledgments
The author and publisher are grateful to the following for permission to reproduce copyright material: ©Alamy **pp. 4** Bottom Right, **12** (Vick Fisher), **6, 22a** (stock shots by itani), **8** (Robert Tunstall), **16** (Digital Vision), **21** (The Garden Picture Library), **22b** (Digital Vision); ©Corbis **p. 11** (Royalty Free); ©Getty Images **pp. 14, 23** (Mike Kelly), **17** (Norbert Wu); ©istockphoto **pp. 4** Top Left, **5** Top Left, **18, 22c** (Moritz von Hacht); ©Jupiter Images **pp. 5** Bottom Right, **20, 22d** (Turner Forte Photography); ©Shutterstock **pp. 4** Bottom Center (RexRover), **4** Bottom Left (Maceofoto), **4** Top Right (Joshua Haviv), **5** Bottom Center, **19** (WizData, inc.), **5** Bottom Left (Jose Fuente), **5** Top Center (Martin Nemec), **5** Top Right (Nadina), **7** (Trutta55), **9** (Elena Elisseeva), **10** (Anette Linnea Rasmussen), **13** (CHUA KOK BENG MARCUS); ©SuperStock **pp. 4** Top Center, **15** (Photographers Choice RF).

Cover photograph reproduced with permission of ©Corbis/Visuals Unlimited.

Back cover photograph reproduced with permission of ©Shutterstock/ Joshua Haviv.

The publishers would like to thank Nancy Harris for her assistance in the preparation of this book.

Every effort has been made to contact copyright holders of any material reproduced in this book. Any omissions will be rectified in subsequent printings if notice is given to the publisher.

Disclaimer
All the Internet addresses (URLs) given in this book were valid at the time of going to press. However, due to the dynamic nature of the Internet, some addresses may have changed, or sites may have changed or ceased to exist since publication. While the author and publisher regret any inconvenience this may cause readers, no responsibility for any such changes can be accepted by either the author or the publisher.

Contents

Violet

Are all plants violet?

Are all animals violet?

Are all rocks violet?

Are all grasses violet?

Plants

Some leaves are violet.

Some leaves are not violet.

Some stems are violet.

Some stems are not violet.

Some flowers are violet.

Some flowers are not violet.

Animals

Some feathers are violet.

Some feathers are not violet.

Some scales are violet.

Some scales are not violet.

Some skin is violet.

Some skin is not violet.

Rocks

Some rocks are violet.

Some rocks are not violet.

Grasses

Some grasses are violet.

Some grasses are not violet.

What Have You Learned?

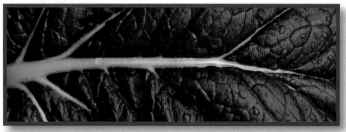 Some plants are violet.

 Some animals are violet.

 Some rocks are violet.

 Some grasses are violet.

Picture Glossary

 **scale** small plate that covers the body of some animals

Index

Note to Parents and Teachers

Before reading:
Talk with children about colors. Explain that there are many different colors, and that each color has a name. Use a color wheel or other simple color chart to point to name each color. Then, ask children to make a list of the colors they can see. After they have completed their list, ask children to share their results.

After reading:
Explain to children that secondary colors (orange, green, and violet) are created by mixing two primary colors. Show children that violet is made from red and blue. Using finger paints, either show the children what red and blue look like when mixed, or encourage the children to mix the paints themselves.